# Guilty feeling

## What is it and how to overcome it?

## Marcus W Oliver

### Editorial Anuket

**Content:**

**Introduction**

# Introduction

*"Until you can say "no," your "yes" is meaningless..."*
(Osho)

The feeling of guilt is a complex and self-reflective emotion that alerts us that "something is wrong" in our behavior. Guilt can be conscious or unconscious, and in both cases, it derives from the conflict between the superego (moral values) and infantile sexual and aggressive desires (the most primitive), a conflict that is an internalized representation and a perpetuation of the conflicts between the child and his parents.

Guilt can manifest itself in a variety of ways, and symptoms can vary from person to person. For some, the feeling of guilt is a vague but continuous sensation: they feel inadequate, and they are at fault, although they do not know why; They feel intimidated, insecure, and scared and end up alone within the walls of the house or with very few and select people. For others, however, guilt manifests itself in more explicit ways, and they are the ones who exaggerate, become inflamed, and feel attacked for nothing, roaring like beasts and then, a moment later, regret it, feel "disgusting", and wonder what they will think. others, try to take refuge or worse yet provoke devious attempts to "maintain the point" that they know is wrong.

In psychology, guilt is worked through cognitive-behavioral therapy (CBT). CBT focuses on identifying the negative thoughts and irrational beliefs that underlie guilt and replacing them with more realistic and positive thoughts. CBT can also help people develop skills to manage anxiety and stress, which can reduce the intensity of guilt.

Determining how guilt is formed, what the negative consequences are, and how these situations can be dealt with is the purpose of this book, which can help those who suffer from it exaggeratedly, mitigate it, and achieve a full life without so many regrets.

# Chapter 1
# What is guilt?

Guilt is a pervasive emotion that, if not resolved, can damage a person's psychological and spiritual development. Classical guilt is defined as "self-reproach for things done or not done," and "feelings of deserving punishment." Guilt is generated by the conflict between the idea of how a person should act and how he or she acts. Guilt can be real or imagined. Blame may not be limited to a specific action or event, but may be vague and indefinite.

Guilt almost always has a strong social context. Historical, religious, and ideological customs constantly change and influence the culturally transmitted experience of guilt. However, guilt is not a universal feeling: what makes one person feel guilty may not make another feel the same way at all.

**What is guilt in psychology?**

Psychology has studied guilt a lot. Sigmund Freud (1856-1939) believed that we feel guilty when there is a gap between our moral conscience (Super Ego) and our innate desires and impulses (Unconscious). He believed that neurotic guilt is the main factor in all psychological problems. In his opinion, the feeling of guilt is always negative and is experienced as an internal conflict, one of whose main objectives is self-punishment. "Motivated" by feelings of guilt, we act in ways that prevent us from doing certain things we consider wrong (lying) and force us to do things we consider right."

Carl Gustav Jung (1875-1961) wrote about the feeling of guilt as a fundamental mechanism for regulating behavior within the framework of accepted moral and ethical standards. At the same time, Jung described the possibility of "good guilt" when a person, being "bad at the moment," chooses to free themselves from "oppressive rules" and new decisions that lead to their personal growth. For example, the decision to leave a failed marriage, the refusal to follow the rules of totalitarian societies that force you to remain committed no matter what the cost.

However, as research progressed, psychologists began to define guilt in other ways. Helen Block Lewis (1913-1987) wrote a landmark book, "Shame and Guilt in Neurosis" (1971), which argued that guilt can have positive consequences, in contrast to guilt-related shame. Her research promoted the idea that "rather than motivating the desire to hide (as in the case of shame), guilt typically motivates reparative behavior: confessing, apologizing, or otherwise making amends for the harm caused."

From a psychosynthetic perspective, anger and guilt arise from unmet expectations toward others and oneself. A victim of a violent crime, for example, may expect that she "should" have avoided the situation or behaved differently to avoid the abuse or attack. Anger toward the aggressor turns into anger toward oneself and leads to intense guilt.

This guilt becomes a complex issue when a person recovers from a traumatic event. And it is possible to free yourself from it only by freeing yourself from unrealistic expectations, both about yourself and others. In many cases, such expectations are associated with traumatized parts of the personality or subpersonalities.

Existentialists see guilt not as a neurotic trait dating back to early childhood (a personality one should not have), but as a personal feeling of "missed opportunities in life." Additionally, there is a transpersonal perspective that may view guilt as a response to a signal from the "wise self" that alerts the individual to take a closer look at her thoughts, motives, and actions.

That said, while guilt can have a positive motivating effect, feeling too much guilt is associated with several mental health problems. This feeling can be a symptom of depression, anxiety disorders, and post-traumatic stress disorder (PTSD). The higher the level of guilt, the more serious the patient's condition. Treatment progress is often associated with a decrease in guilt.

Guilt itself is a contributing factor to the development of a wide range of mental problems, such as depression (which psychoanalysts consider frozen anger), sleep disturbances, fatigue, compulsive overeating, destructive sexual behavior, and substance addiction.

**What is not the fault**

Now that we know what guilt is, it is important to understand what it is not. Guilt is often confused with the related emotion of shame, but they are completely different emotions. Both emotions are self-centered, meaning they make us think more and more about ourselves. However, guilt focuses on action, while shame focuses on issues of identity and self-esteem. When we feel shame, we feel that our actions make us "bad" people. When we feel guilty, we feel that what we did was wrong. In other words, guilt does not threaten our core identity," but shame does pose a serious threat to it.

These two feelings also often lead to very different actions: guilt can allow social relationships to be repaired and suffocated by remedying and compensating for the damage caused, while shame disrupts socialization as the person withdraws into themselves. Shame is associated with self-directed anger and guilt with empathy.


**Can guilt be a good thing?**

Because it is an unpleasant feeling, guilt has a bad reputation. However psychological research shows that feeling guilty can prompt us to engage in positive behavior. Guilt is associated with helping behavior; When we feel guilty, we are more likely to help someone else. Feeling guilty can also make us more honest. Additionally, feelings of guilt can make us more prone to empathy: sympathy, and the ability to understand other people's feelings and points of view. When we feel empathy, we are more likely to help someone and be less angry with them. Research has shown that when we feel guilt (rather than shame), we feel more empathy for the person we have wronged.

However, the mere presence of a feeling of guilt can be an indulgence and at the same time a "payment" not to change anything: "I suffer from guilt, that's enough."

# Chapter 2
# Guilt in childhood

## Why does guilt arise?

It is believed that at an unconscious level, self-accusations can already occur in a baby, that is, this mechanism is familiar to us from those moments when we could not express something in words or fully understand what was happening. With the advent of mature thinking, the tool of "guilt" becomes even more convenient to use.

For a young child, parents are a bastion of security, strength, and stability. They guarantee their survival and development. Unconsciously, babies and young children implicitly trust their parents' authority. But if for some reason a child suffers from his parents' behavior, he faces a dilemma: who is wrong? Is it his all-powerful parents, whom he still adores and reveres unconditionally, or is the problem with himself? In order not to disturb the stability of his existence, the child unconsciously blames himself for the fact that something went wrong between him and his parents. In some situations, this attitude remains in a person for many years and can dictate his line of behavior.

The good news is that psychotherapy helps to overcome this problem and stop living according to the pattern of a traumatic event that has settled in the unconscious. Contrary to rumors, psychotherapy is not designed to penetrate every corner of the subconscious and reach childhood memories. Often it is enough to pay attention to the external manifestations of the problem to get closer to understanding the causes of guilt, solving them, and changing behavior to a prosperous and productive one.

Dealing with feelings of guilt involves developing new and healthy habits in the perception of reality and behavior.


## Guilt complex

A guilt complex occurs when a person has the constant belief that he has done, is doing, or will do something wrong. A guilt complex can arise from imagined or perceived guilt. This worldview may be the result of an upbringing in which the child was made to feel guilty for normal experiences such as sadness, anger, or normal developmental needs (e.g., exploring one's genitals, engaging in self-gratification, showing interest in the opposite sex), etc.).

Guilt can also arise when you are blamed for things that are actually out of your control or for which others are responsible. For example, in the case of "birth guilt," the mother instills in the child that he is to blame for having suffered during childbirth or for her husband abandoning the family because of her birth.

Very often, feelings of guilt arise due to violation of irrational parental instructions: "Don't feel", "Don't come close", "Don't be smart", etc. Using blame is one of the most common ways to manipulate others to get them to act a certain way or take a certain action. This is a special type of intimidation and manipulation tactic that keeps people trapped in a state of uncertainty and anxiety. The most prominent example is the use of "original sin" or the concept of sins to manipulate the flock of religious organizations.


**Formation of feelings of guilt**

A child learns the meaning of moral and ethical standards from his parents. Researchers say this starts to happen as early as 3 years of age. One theory that may help explain where guilt comes from is Erik Erikson's (1902-1994) eight stages of psychosexual development. It is in the third stage where he explains where our feelings of guilt come from. This stage, "initiative versus guilt," refers to the preschool age: 4 to 5 years. At this stage, we take the initiative and learn new things. We begin to control ourselves more and interact with more people in new social settings. As we learn from these social interactions, we are encouraged to take more initiative, we judge that we have failed, or we are told so. If we perceive failure, we feel bad and can develop guilt.

A modern psychological model suggests that guilt arises from the following elements:

• Feel responsible for what happened
• Feelings of violation of your standards or values.
• There are no excuses for what was done (or not done).

The guilt symptom complex includes:

• **Emotional component**: depression, suffering.
• **Cognitive component:** analysis of action or inaction, awareness of the conflict between "should" and what was "done", regret and remorse, low self-esteem.
• **Motivational component:** desire to correct or compensate for what has been done.
• **Psychosomatic component:** headaches, sleep disturbances, heaviness of the stomach.

The sources of feelings of guilt without any real reason are:

Parental instructions, for example, "You are a bad girl, daughter...". Parents use this guilt as a means of psychological control of children. Such guilt, since it cannot be redeemed in ordinary life (due to the accepted introject of the persecuting (guilty) parent), is passed down from generation to generation, serving as the basis for transgenerational trauma.

The parental order "Do not live" can manifest itself in the form of guilt for the birth, which the child assumes:

• Guilt for the fact of being born ("If it weren't for you, I...")
• Guilt over a premature birth ("It's your fault I didn't graduate from college")
• Guilt for being born into the wrong sex ("They wanted a boy, but you are a girl")
• Guilt for a wrong birth (cesarean section, etc.)

Imaginary existential guilt is only a form of self-punishment and does not encourage the person to develop. This is the fault:

• To yourself for insufficient achievements ("I haven't achieved everything I should")
• In front of others for insufficient service ("What have you done for the country?")
• Before God ("I have not served the Almighty enough")
• Imaginary guilt of hyperresponsibility, for example, guilt for others living poorly (guilt for starving children in Africa, endangered animals, etc.), which may be a manifestation of Rescuer syndrome.


## Imaginary survivor's guilt

"Survivor guilt can be experienced by people who have witnessed the death of others and survived." A special form of survivor guilt is missing twin syndrome guilt, in which the surviving sibling experiences unexplained feelings of guilt. Rumination is one of the key parts of survivor's guilt. Ruminating is thinking over and over again about an event that becomes persistent and distracts from the present moment. Rumination is also a factor in other mental health problems, such as the development of depression and anxiety. In many ways, survivor guilt is an undue burden because often the outcome of a traumatic event cannot be changed.

## Imaginary associative guilt

Associative guilt is "responsibility for a crime" that is imposed on an innocent person solely because he or she has some connection to the actual culprit. In other words, we may hold people guilty or ourselves guilty simply because we have a connection to someone who did (or failed to do) something bad. For example, members of the white population in the United States may feel guilt toward African Americans because of their slave-owning past.

## A person who tries to please everyone

Have you ever done something you didn't want to do? Have you ever changed your mind just because someone didn't like it? If your answer is yes, then you are the type of person who can or is used to pleasing others. In any case, if you are willing to submit to other people's opinions or positions without any justification or compelling reason, then you are most likely trying to please someone. A person who is condescending to people will do anything to please others, whether they ask him to or the person himself "understands" what people want from him. Such a person places himself on a lower level than others, giving priority to other important people (both in positive and negative terms) to him.

## What is behind pleasant behavior?

To some, people pleasers seem like the kindest and friendliest. Many even try to imitate them. But in reality, it is very difficult to be a nice person, because in his life there is no place for him, his opinion, and his own "I".

Sometimes we wonder how someone can be so selfless, dedicating their entire life and interests to others. These people certainly have their own opinions, tastes, and thoughts, but they always try to adapt and change them to please others.

The root of self-sacrifice lies in the fact that such people lack confidence in life and crave external support. Your basic need for security and self-esteem is based solely on the approval of other people.

This behavior is typical of traumatized people who feel victimized and decide to renounce their self, their true nature, and their identity, to receive confirmation of their value by serving others: partner, husband, star, boss, party, religion. This is the typical model of survival for a traumatized soul through the Rescue: by relating to others it is easier to distance oneself from oneself and one's traumas and unresolved problems.

Their low self-esteem is temporarily corrected when, by serving, pleasing, or doing "the right thing," they become submissive to the will and interests of others, receiving in return explicit or hidden (and sometimes fanciful) rewards and reinforcements for their self-esteem. Often this behavior leads to codependent relationships.

Another reason for pleasure and rescue may be the models of obligation instilled by parents. These situations are observed when a child is born with a specific objective: "You must strengthen our marriage", "You must make us happy", or "You must return the investment we have made in you". "Living for oneself is a sin. We must live for others, as our religion teaches!

Constantly living in such a distorted world, these people begin to believe that, first of all, they should value, respect, and fulfill the wishes of other people or groups of people (for example, the customs of their community), and not their own. own. Pleasers are always very worried and anxious that others will reject or exclude them if they do not behave according to other people's expectations. People who please themselves in this way constantly fear that they will not be loved if they stop pleasing the interests of others. Thanks to this situation, people-pleasers are always in a state of chronic stress and anxiety. When doing things for themselves (which they sometimes have to do to support their own lives), pleasers experience anxiety and worry that they are doing something wrong. To calm themselves, they work to regain the approval of their loved ones, hoping to bolster their self-esteem and reduce the anxiety associated with their agreeable behavior.

When these expectations are violated, which happens quite often, because others can quickly tire of the pleasant and flattering, clearly insincere style of behavior, the pleaser becomes even more restless and anxious, chaotically directing his efforts to obtain approval. Such a vicious circle leads to an increase in internal tension and, ultimately, to a deterioration in the adaptive capabilities of the psyche and the body as a whole. This condition can manifest itself in increased irritability, depression, sleep disturbances, increased blood pressure, heart pain, headaches, and digestive disorders.

## What does it mean to please people?

Being a person who wants to please others means having little self-confidence. When we strive to love and appreciate, to please and obey everyone around us, this means that, above all, we want others to show the attention, care, and love that we are deprived of. The desire to please and do good to others is a sure sign of a lack of self-love. At the same time, constant preoccupation with pleasing others in the vain hope of receiving love and recognition in return deprives the person of strength, creates great tension, and is a great waste of time and energy.

Wanting to gain approval, a person may run from one place to another, adapting to the opinions and needs of different people. This process can be endless and simply exhausting; After all, it's impossible to please everyone at once. What you do may please one person, but anger or irritate another. These things will leave you dissatisfied and put you in a state of hopelessness and worthlessness because your only strategy for coping with the world around you is not working as well as you would like, greatly reducing your self-esteem.

## People with low self-esteem are targets of manipulators

People with low self-esteem often become dependent on exploiters and manipulators who take advantage of such unhappy people for their ends, reinforcing their low self-esteem. For example, by relying on people with low self-esteem, totalitarian regimes, and sects implement their ideological doctrines.

These people, with the help of the media and ideologized art, in collective suggestion sessions (party meetings, team building, sessions) are constantly taught that the person himself and his interests are not important "for the common cause", and only the total renunciation of their interests and objectives for the "common good" or the "great idea", the subordination of will and interests to the "collective", the "majority" or the "leader". People who depend on the opinions of others, with virtually no violence or material incentives, can make infinite "passes," support the "general party line," vote "correctly" in elections, and all other possible types of unrequited delegation of powers. his will.

# Chapter 3
# Guilt, anxiety, and depression

Feelings of guilt can be the cause of self-doubt, anxiety, dissatisfaction with others, and life in general.

Guilt is a negative attitude in which we feel that our actions are the cause of others or our misfortunes. This feeling has a variety of manifestations and is not always directly related to being responsible for some mistake. This feeling can arise in any situation where there has been severe stress (in the language of psychology, trauma).

Having arisen in the human psyche, this unpleasant feeling performs an important function: it helps to adapt to a difficult situation to survive with less damage: instead of focusing on the traumatic situation, we look at the feeling of guilt, because "It doesn't hurt that much" and requires less internal work. We can say that the feeling of guilt itself is almost accidental and any other negative attitude could have formed in its place. For example; Let's say you were a 7-year-old boy, who suddenly stared at a 32-year-old woman; and the lady's husband, noticing this fact, and wanting to be funny, looks you straight in the eyes and with a threatening voice says, "Why are you looking at my wife, do you like her?!" Remember, you are 7 years old, and you know little about complex adult humor, and you take those words as a serious warning that you have done something wrong. Your brain, not very mature to interpret the facts and even less mature to find a solution, makes you feel guilty for having done something wrong; and the proof is that you received a reprimand from someone who is supposedly a source of truth. The trauma originates right there, and when you become an adult, whenever you are interested in a woman, you try to avoid looking directly at her, since your brain remembers when you were repressed. It doesn't matter that you can now rationalize the events of childhood, since what your brain tries to do is avoid the discomfort you received that time, and returns again and again to repeat the childish solution that you used: the feeling of guilt.

## The intricate dance between guilt and anxiety: a vicious cycle that affects your well-being

Guilt and anxiety are two emotions that dance together in a vicious circle, feeding each other and creating an emotional burden that can significantly affect our well-being.

## Guilt as origin

Guilt arises from the perception of having done something wrong or not having met expectations. It may be real or imaginary, but its impact on the person is real.

Feeling guilty can cause:
• **Negative thoughts:** Self-criticism, rumination on the past, fear of punishment.
• **Emotions:** Sadness, shame, low self-esteem.

- **Behaviors:** Self-punishment, social isolation, avoidance.
- **Anxiety as a consequence**

In another, not-so-obvious way, guilt finds its way out through great anxiety.

At some point in our lives, we all experience anxiety: due to illnesses of loved ones, at work, in conflicts with colleagues, when we hear sad news, etc. However, a healthy person's anxiety is proportional to the situation and disappears over time.

High anxiety is a wide range of painful conditions that are difficult to control and sometimes difficult to track ("Something torments me, although objectively everything is fine in life").

High anxiety can lead to health problems, the cause of which doctors cannot find, sleeping problems, "unreasonable" mood swings, overeating, or, conversely, obsession with dieting, overwork, or loss of strength. Anxiety has many symptoms, and if any of them sound familiar to you, then this is a reason to think about the reasons.

The subconscious can choose anxiety as a channel through which tension comes out of the main problem: feelings of guilt. This happens when it is so unbearable or such a difficult experience is associated with it that the psyche refuses to even look in that direction and tries to control at least what it can control. This is how anxiety appears: an object of anxiety is selected and all forces are directed to combat it.

Guilt can trigger anticipatory anxiety about the possible consequences of the mistake or the fear of being judged.

The person worries excessively about the future and experiences:

• **Physical symptoms:** Restlessness, sweating, palpitations, difficulty breathing.
• **Cognitive symptoms:** Catastrophic thoughts, difficulty concentrating, irritability.
• **Behaviors:** Avoidance of situations that generate anxiety, seeking excessive control.

A vicious circle:

Anxiety in turn can increase guilt, as the person may feel responsible for their symptoms or for not being able to control their anxiety.

This creates a negative spiral that can be difficult to break on your own.

**How to break the cycle**

• **Identify the root of the guilt:** Is it real or imaginary? Is it based on facts or irrational beliefs?
• **Manage anxiety:** Practice relaxation techniques, mindfulness, and cognitive-behavioral therapy.
• **Learn to forgive yourself:** Accept mistakes as part of learning and focus on the present.
• **Develop healthy self-esteem:** Recognize strengths and accept weaknesses.

• **Seek professional help:** If guilt and anxiety interfere with daily life, it is important to seek help from a psychologist or therapist.

It is a complex construct and to eradicate anxiety, the root cause needs to be addressed. It is much easier to do it together with a psychologist. So if you're familiar with anxiety but don't know what causes it, talk to a specialist. This mechanism will be familiar to you and you will quickly find the solution to your painful condition. Furthermore, the therapist is free of his feelings of guilt, he does not follow his rules, and contact with someone who does not follow the rules of guilt is in itself very useful.

Remember: Guilt and anxiety are normal emotions, but they don't have to control you. With the right knowledge and tools, you can break the vicious cycle and enjoy better emotional well-being.

## Guilt and Depression: A Toxic Duo

Guilt and depression are two emotions that dance together in an emotional tango, feeding each other in a vicious cycle that can be difficult to break. Guilt can be a symptom of depression, but it can also be a factor that triggers or makes it worse.

## Guilt in Depression:

• Negative thoughts: The person with depression blames himself for real or imagined mistakes, exaggerating his responsibility for negative events.
• Self-criticism: Judges herself harshly, ruminating on past mistakes and feeling unworthy of forgiveness.
• Low self-esteem: Guilt erodes self-esteem, making the person see themselves as a failure and worthless.

## How guilt makes depression worse:

• **Isolation:** Shame and guilt can lead the person to isolate themselves socially, avoiding contact with friends and family.
• **Hopelessness:** Feeling guilty for not "getting better" can fuel hopelessness and the feeling that depression is permanent.
• **Demotivation:** Guilt can sap energy and motivation to do activities that were previously enjoyed.

## Breaking the Vicious Circle:

• **Therapy:** Cognitive behavioral therapy can help identify distorted thought patterns related to guilt and develop strategies to challenge them.
• **Self-compassion:** Learning to treat yourself with kindness and understanding, rather than self-criticism, is essential for recovery.
• **Forgiveness:** Forgiving yourself for past mistakes does not mean forgetting, but rather accepting what cannot be changed and moving forward.

**Tips for managing Guilt:**

• **Distinguish between real and unfounded guilt:** Not all guilt is valid. Analyze the situation objectively to determine if blame is justified.
• **Learn to forgive yourself:** Forgiveness is not easy, but it is crucial for healing. Practice self-compassion and recognize that we all make mistakes.
• **Share the burden:** Talking to a friend, family member, or therapist about your feelings of guilt can help you feel less alone and get support.

**Remember:** Guilt is not a sign of weakness, but a common symptom of depression. If guilt is gripping you, seek professional help. With the right treatment, you can break the vicious cycle and find your way to recovery.

# Chapter 4
# Guilt and shame.
# Self-esteem and self-love

**Guilt and shame: what's the difference?**

First of all, guilt is one of the human feelings, an integral part of our life. It is not as simple and obvious as joy, anger, or pain. Rather, it can be attributed to more complex experiences such as disappointment or gratitude.

Guilt is always a negative reaction; It is unproductive and even destructive. In essence, it is aggression directed at oneself: self-humiliation, self-flagellation, and the desire for self-punishment.

Almost always a person feels guilty for not having been able to change or avoid something. It must be understood: that there is a big difference between "being guilty" and "feeling guilty." A person is guilty if he has deliberately caused harm. Likewise, the one who caused harm, but could not do anything else, or the one who did not cause any harm, but still feels responsible, may feel guilty.

There is also another verbal confusion: in colloquial speech, people often confuse the concepts of "guilt", "conscience", "responsibility" and "shame" and use them as synonyms. They say: "Aren't you ashamed, don't you feel responsible, don't you have a conscience, don't you feel guilty?", as if they were the same thing.

**What is the fundamental difference?**

Consciousness and responsibility are useful, productive, and appropriate feelings, but guilt is not.

Consciousness is an internal self-control that evaluates the actions taken. It encourages you to follow moral standards and helps you be responsible.

Responsibility is the voluntary agreement to care for oneself and others. Feeling responsible means trying to fulfill all obligations and, in case of failure, being willing to admit a mistake, correct it, and do everything possible to avoid doing something similar in the future.

**How to distinguish guilt from other experiences?**

The feeling of guilt is experienced as a problem. If you feel bad, you suffer in a self-destructive way, that means you are experiencing exactly that. You will notice that you focus too much on your thoughts, and mistakes and torment yourself. You will feel unworthy and have no right to anything.

Pains of conscience and responsibility for mistakes, in turn, are never experienced as destructive and fruitless suffering. On the contrary, they ennoble a person, push him to a new level of development, and help him live according to principles.

What about shame? Is this also a positive feeling?

No, shame, like guilt, is negative and destructive.

This is a very difficult and painful experience: a person experiences it when he is helpless. As a rule, shame is associated with a hopeless situation that cannot be influenced, for example, by psychological trauma due to experienced violence.

Shame is a very early experience. This is one of the basic effects: very young children experience it for the first time when someone violates their boundaries and free will. For example, older children take away a toy. The baby cannot resist them and feels helpless.

Interestingly, often, in order not to feel shame, a person is more willing to experience feelings of guilt.

The point is that shame is impotent ("I couldn't do anything, I was helpless") and guilt seems powerful ("I could, but I didn't"). A person admits the idea that he could have acted differently and feels tormented. Although in most cases it is just an illusion.


**Reasons to feel guilty**

Blame has three main sources. Each is independent in itself and exists separately, but often a combination of all of them is found.

It first arises from childhood. As we have mentioned previously, a child first experiences feelings of guilt between three and five years of age. The initial objective is psychological protection against the terrifying feeling of helplessness. The fact is that it is during this period that the boy's omnipotence complex collapses: he begins to realize that he is neither immortal nor omnipotent and he is weak in many ways.

The child internally clings to the feeling of guilt as a way of preserving the image of his omnipotence. He seems to say to himself: "It turns out I can't do everything. It is unbearable! Although no, most likely I was wrong and I am still omnipotent, but this time it didn't work. I could, but I didn't try. Guilty. Next time maybe I can."

Erik Erikson defines the period of three to five years as the third phase of human development called "Creative Initiative or Guilt." In favorable family conditions, the child gradually accepts his "non-omnipotence" and overcomes feelings of guilt: the dilemma is resolved in favor of the successful development of creative initiative. If things are unfavorable, creative initiative, on the other hand, is limited. The boy grows up, but the weight of guilt continues to interfere with his life.

The second source is related to post-traumatic stress. When we go through a difficult situation (the death of a loved one, or our parents' divorce), we feel guilt; This is one of the mandatory phases of processing a traumatic experience. Although in reality the event and its outcome did not depend on us. If you do not go through this phase of experiencing the pain of loss to the end, the feeling of guilt will persist for the rest of your life.

The third source of guilt is transgenerational. In simple words, it is when parents and grandparents, through experience, words, and behavior, "inherit" us with their sense of guilt.

**How does guilt develop in childhood?**

**What should parents do so that their children can successfully say goodbye to feelings of guilt?**

Stop blaming the children. It is the constant reproaches, belittling, and scolding of the family that do not allow children to overcome the feeling of guilt at five or six years old. Parents often use guilt as a parenting tool. They believe that in this way they cultivate awareness and responsibility in the child, replacing concepts that we have already talked about.

Parents place blame on the child and use it as a whip, inciting him to act. Often this happens not because of bad intentions, but simply because the adults themselves do not know how to do the opposite: they were once brought up in the same way.

The child is not able to think critically and takes all of the parents' actions at face value. He doesn't realize where the truth is and where it isn't, and he believes everything he hears: that he is guilty, that he deserves blame, that he is responsible for his actions.

But the truth is that a small child is not yet able to take responsibility for his actions, so scolding and blaming him is meaningless. He is a priori innocent:

even if he has broken a glass vase, even if he has gone for a walk alone or has dirty something new. Only the parents are responsible: they overlooked, did not explain, and did not remove the vase from the edge.

Young children are impulsive: they do not yet see cause-and-effect relationships and do not measure their efforts. Adults attribute psychological abilities to them that have not yet been formed.

## What to replace the charges with? How to talk to a child?

It is necessary to explain with patience, calm, and consistency that any action has a result and correct errors. Such a sincere dialogue, although difficult, will awaken empathy and conscience in the child, not guilt.

## How to get rid of guilt?

Guilt greatly reduces the quality of life. By being cruel and unfair, it deprives one of self-confidence and reduces self-esteem. A person cannot defend his interests, poorly protects personal boundaries, and punishes himself for any crime. Those around him easily take strings from him and manipulate him in every possible way.

Guilt consumes a lot of energy and exhausts. It brings a constant feeling of heaviness and pain, disappointment and dejection. Many people stop enjoying life and do not allow themselves any pleasure.

## How does guilt feel on a bodily level?

First, changes in posture: the person seems to feel a heavy load on his shoulders and bends under the weight of it. Then the gait becomes forced, the head tilts more and more, and the corners of the mouth droop.

"Guilty" is easy to judge by appearance. Among people with chronic feelings of guilt, problems with the seventh cervical vertebra are very common.

## Why is one's own will to overcome guilt not enough?

Let's say you call your mom and she tells you that she's been waiting for your call all day and that now her heart hurts. You feel guilty. Stimulated by this feeling, you will call her every day, and if you don't call, you will most likely hear: "Don't you care about your mother? ... Don't you care that she makes me feel so bad? "

The feeling of guilt in this case will become your red button, a thread that your mother will pull. You will not be able to stop this painful cycle because of an emotional connection. She may be healthy all this time.

When working with feelings of guilt, the most important part of therapists' work focuses on the cognitive sphere. We need to get rid of false beliefs formed in childhood. Discovering exactly how they pressed your feelings of guilt, finding this "record" and eliminating it is the goal.

In psychodrama, a scene from childhood is represented in which a person feels guilty and is looked at from the outside. An adult perspective helps to understand the situation and dismantle false beliefs.

For example, you broke a vase and were accused of being careless. We must replace the false perception ("it's your fault") with an appropriate one ("the father should have removed the vase from the child's field of vision"). A scene from childhood is depicted, after which the patient is asked to look in the mirror like an adult and ask: "Do you think the child was guilty of what he was accused of?"

## Collective guilt: can this happen?

For a morally mature and psychologically healthy person, feelings of guilt do not exist. There is only awareness and a sense of responsibility for each step taken, for making decisions, for choosing, and for rejecting them.

A mistake made does not horrify a mature person, it does not exhaust him internally: he simply corrects it and moves on. If correction is impossible, learn your lesson and don't make similar mistakes in the future. This is an adult position.

And pouring ashes on your head, considering yourself bad, and scolding yourself for what you have done and not done is the behavior of a defenseless child.

And in cases of collective feelings of guilt that appear in people in the context of global events?

You simply have to separate yourself from that feeling and not participate in it. It is important to understand: that collective guilt is a priori false. There is no general responsibility, it is always personal: we are responsible only for ourselves and never for a larger group.

If you are accused of something collectively, as a community or nation, ask yourself the question: "What could I personally do to correct the situation? And could it? Most likely, it will turn out that the outcome was not up to you in any of the scenarios.

You can grieve, feel helpless, worry, and sympathize, but all of these feelings have nothing to do with guilt. Learn to separate accusations from your real responsibility.


**Self-esteem: what it is and how to increase it**

In psychology, self-love is, above all, self-care. Care is the ability to observe one's feelings, desires, and needs.

Let's look at an example: Suppose you have a controversial situation at work, which may be your fault. How will you feel and how will you act?

You will immediately begin to regret it, apologize, take full responsibility, and eventually go home feeling like you are a bad employee. And to fix it all, you will refuse to rest.

Take a break and figure out the problem. If it turns out that you have a responsibility, admit it and offer ways out of this situation. At the same time, ask your colleagues for help if you need it, and don't deprive yourself of rest and weekends.

The first option is a useless method of self-flagellation, which can harm well-being and is unlikely to help effectively cope with difficulties. The second option is to take care of yourself. You treat yourself with care, you notice not only your flaws but also your strengths, and you accept yourself and skillfully manage your emotions.

**What is self-love based on?**

Personality consists of three interacting parts.

• The vulnerable part, let's call it "the child". She is responsible for emotions and experiences.
• Inner critic, who constantly tries to regulate our emotions and actions by attacking, blaming, and devaluing us.

• And the third part is a healthy adult, or a loving parent, who supports the childish part of our personality and protects it from destructive criticism.

And to love yourself you need:

Satisfy all the basic needs of the inner child. Treat yourself with compassion. Understand what the inner child is missing. The list of basic emotional needs looks like this:

• Security, secure attachment, and acceptance of others. Trust in at least one person strengthens your inner support.
• Autonomy, independence. They are usually missing in those who, as children, were not allowed to try new things or do what they liked. Sometimes this unmet need turns into a constant desire to demonstrate to everyone your abilities and skills. And sometimes even a complete denial of autonomy, even in adulthood.
• Spontaneity and play. Lack of preparation for sudden changes in plans, and devaluation of sudden desires take away flexibility and openness to new experiences.
• Freedom to express needs and emotions. It is important to be in a place where all feelings are acceptable. Repressing them also represses us.

If you have made enough effort to take care of your basic emotional needs, then you have taken care of your self-esteem. And you are no longer in danger. This is the state of a happy child. Additionally, it includes the state of a healthy adult, which metaphorically reflects our ability to show care, and compassion, set boundaries, and know the desires and capabilities of our inner child.

## How to increase self-esteem

The level of self-esteem depends directly on love/hatred for oneself. Therefore, by mastering the skill of self-care, you automatically work on self-esteem.

## Step 1
## Accept what cannot be changed
Acceptance is not about despair or a passive attitude towards life. This is a refusal to fight reality. The more useless the struggle with what cannot be changed, the stronger the feeling of helplessness; This is precisely what causes the feeling of self-loathing. For example, it is impossible to change the past. You must accept it and, from that moment on, start acting differently.

Developing the ability to accept is not easy, but it is an important step toward self-care skills. When we do not accept what cannot be changed, we experience helplessness and despair, and our self-esteem plummets. Therefore, learning to accept reality means learning to move forward, filling your life with compassion and self-care. These are all functions of a healthy adult.

## Step 2
## Prepare for what life has to offer.
This skill is closely related to acceptance. By accepting even the most unpleasant reality, one accepts oneself in it and prepares oneself for challenges.

Goodwill presupposes full participation in one's own life and responsibility for it. The more one realizes that he is the master of his life, the stronger the inner support and the higher the self-esteem. This determines how successfully you will face crises.

## Step 3
## Be open

New bad experiences and negative comments should not undermine self-love. Openness is psychological flexibility, the ability to meet fear halfway. Don't focus on mistakes, but rather on understanding what skill is needed to improve the situation you are in.

Openness is associated with psychological well-being, with our ability to learn new things. In other words, the lower the level of openness, the fewer social connections, the smaller the range of interests, the smaller the development horizon, and the more tasks we cannot cope with.

## How to learn to take care of yourself - 3 exercises

Self-care can be learned. Let's look at three practices that will help you take better care of yourself.

### • Practice the "swing"

Thanks to this exercise you will understand what your inner child needs to be happy.

Close your eyes and imagine a tree with a swing on which a small, sad child is sitting. Are you? Imagine that you approach the child and reflect on why he is sad, and what is bothering him.

Next, think about how he wants to help: hug, talk, encourage.

This exercise will help you feel two states at once: a child and an adult. On the one hand, you may feel unmet basic needs. On the other hand, from the perspective of a healthy adult, you were able to discern these needs, which means you were already cared for and supported.


## • Practice returning to inner wisdom
Everyone has inner wisdom. And feeling it is the first step to taking care of yourself. Sit back, relax, and think about a time last week when you hesitated and couldn't make a decision.

Ask yourself, "How wisely have I acted?" No correction criteria are needed. Check-in with your feelings - internal impulses will tell you the correct answer. If you realize that your action was not entirely correct and hesitate to admit it, try to guess: "Which decision would be wiser?"


## • The practice of radical acceptance
Create the most comfortable environment for you. Think about what life events are difficult for you to accept right now. Write them down. Choose one of them and try to honestly answer the following questions:

• What happens to you when I think about this?
• How did this event occur in my life, in what context did this situation develop?
• What will change in my life if I can accept these circumstances? What will I do first?

Everything has its reasons and they don't always depend on us. It is important to accept reality with both the body and the mind. Try to relax. Say to yourself in a compassionate tone: "Yes, this is how it is, I cannot change this fact of reality." Observe your feelings, leave them alone. Remember right now that although there are facts you cannot change, you are still yourself. Even if you refuse to fight them, you can continue to follow your values and create a life worth enjoying.

Think about what you could do to express your acceptance. Start doing these things gradually. The result of acceptance is always action. Our attitude towards ourselves changes only when we start doing something based on acceptance.

# Chapter 5
# Other manifestations of guilt

**Survivor guilt complex: what is it?**

Many people face a feeling of helplessness and guilt for not being able to contribute significant benefits and help to society.

Those emotions are destructive. They paralyze activity, cause quarrels and conflicts in the family, and people devalue themselves and their actions. This is because the nervous system strives to discharge itself and therefore tries to free itself.

**Survivor's Guilt: Signs**

Survivor syndrome is a specific reaction to traumatic events, a form of post-traumatic stress disorder.

It happens, for example, when people decide to flee war for their safety, to leave the country. Or when they manage to survive and get out of dangerous places, while others are attacked and die. People may also feel guilty because they supposedly did not do enough for others or were unable to change the outcome.

Feelings of guilt can put pressure on people both physically and psychologically, some of its symptoms are:

**Psychological:**
• memories of a dangerous situation, obsessive thoughts;
• nervousness, unconditional anger, mood swings;
• apathy, helplessness, decreased motivation;
• suicidal thoughts.

**Physical symptoms:**
• headache;
• lack of appetite, nausea, stomach or abdominal pain;
• insomnia;
• heart disease.

This syndrome can manifest itself due to various circumstances: moving to another country, staying in a safer place, inability to help. Survivor guilt severely affects a person's life, and their ability to make decisions and evaluate the situation carefully and objectively.


**To do?**

1. Understand that fear for your own life and that of your loved ones, panic, and the desire to leave the country are the first natural reactions. And that's fine. They are automatic and ensure biological survival at an instinctive level.

2. By being safe, you are already doing good. You are a support for those who depend on you: children, seniors, pets. When he is more or less calm, it helps cover his basic needs: sleep, food, water, and health. You can help in other ways, too: volunteering, cooking

for refugees, working to rebuild the economy. So little by little we move on to the next step.

3. By calming down, you will be able to expand your influence. Bring physical help and provide psychological support to those around you (family, neighbors, friends, followers on social networks).

4. If you can, team up with like-minded people. Join a specific activity. As already mentioned above, this can be a voluntary, humanitarian, physical, informational, or any other activity.

5. Continue to be supportive of yourself and those around you. Little by little you will discover how you can be useful, you will see those who need you.

Of course, we understand how difficult it can be to control yourself, especially in such dire circumstances. Everyone needs to understand that they can help anywhere, even if they have to flee war to another country.

## Missing twin syndrome: An unexpected emotional journey

Missing twin syndrome, also known as of the vanishing twin, is an experience that affects a considerable number of twin pregnancies. It is characterized by the loss of one of the fetuses during the early stages of pregnancy, usually before 12 weeks. Although this event may be difficult to cope with emotionally, it is important to understand that it is not the mother's fault and does not affect the chances of a healthy pregnancy in the future.


## What happens in missing twin syndrome?

In a twin pregnancy, two embryos implant in the uterus and begin to develop. However, in some cases, one of the embryos stops growing and is reabsorbed by the mother's body, the placenta, or the other twin. This process usually occurs without the mother experiencing any symptoms and is often discovered during a routine ultrasound.


## What are the causes of missing twin syndrome?

The exact causes of missing twin syndrome are not completely known. However, it is believed that several factors may contribute to fetal loss, including:

• **Chromosomal abnormalities:** The fetus may have chromosomal abnormalities incompatible with life, which can lead to its early death.
• **Placental problems:** A poorly formed placenta or inadequate blood flow can deprive the fetus of the nutrients and oxygen it needs to develop.
• **Infections:** Some infections, such as rubella or cytomegalovirus, can cause fetal death.
• **Environmental factors:** Alcohol, tobacco, or drug use during pregnancy can increase the risk of miscarriage.

**How is missing twin syndrome diagnosed?**

Missing twin syndrome is usually diagnosed during a routine ultrasound. On ultrasound, a single gestational sac with a single viable fetus is observed. In some cases, remains of the missing fetus can be seen, such as a small amorphous mass.

**What are the consequences of missing twin syndrome?**

Missing twin syndrome can have a significant emotional impact on the mother. Feelings of sadness, guilt, anxiety, and uncertainty are common. The mother needs to receive emotional support from her partner, family, friends, or a mental health professional.

**How can you prevent missing twin syndrome?**

There is no sure way to prevent missing twin syndrome. However, women who are planning a pregnancy can take some steps to reduce the risk of miscarriage, such as:

• Eat a healthy and balanced diet.
• Exercise regularly.
• Avoid the consumption of alcohol, tobacco, and drugs.
• Have a regular prenatal check-up.
• The future after missing twin syndrome

Despite the painful experience, most women who experience missing twin syndrome can have a healthy future pregnancy. The mother needs to take the time necessary to heal emotionally before trying to conceive again.


## Feeling guilty about one's success

Joy over the achievements of various people is overshadowed by thoughts about the suffering of loved ones. They begin to doubt that they have the right to feel good when others around them feel bad. These experiences manifest in ways similar to survivor's guilt.

To overcome the guilt of being successful, a person may downplay excellent results, work to exhaustion, or waste large amounts of money for no benefit. People with the following characteristics are often more likely to feel guilty about success:

Low self-esteem: people who admit that they do not feel their worth;

The attitude of "taking everything and dividing it": a person strives to ensure that everything is fair, (without foundations), only then does it seem to him that life is fair;

Black and white thinking: a person believes that they are lucky at the expense of others

Fear of separation: a person wants to be on the same level as their loved ones so that they accept them as one of their own.


**Fear of criticism and condemnation.**

The surest way to avoid criticism and condemnation is to do nothing, hide, and be invisible.

The fear of criticism prevents you from developing in your profession, expressing yourself as a person, or expressing your opinion in the company of friends or with your family. Sometimes this becomes the reason for procrastination, when there is a desire to do something, but something (for example, unconscious fear) always stops it, attention shifts to other, more familiar and easier things.

When expressing ourselves in society, whether speaking in public, interacting with colleagues, and friends, in reality or on the Internet, we can encounter not only a careful and tactful expression of criticism directed at us but also real rudeness or hatred, which we must analyze and give the corresponding importance.


**What's so scary about criticism?**

• I am ashamed of not living up to my ideals,
• Embarrassed in front of parents, teachers, and other people in authority whose opinions are important;

• Fear of rejection, of not being accepted by other people or communities;
• I am afraid that I will not be able to cope with the emotions that arise;
• Fear of the unknown – I don't know what others will say;
• Loss of control – other people's opinions are out of my control.

You will surely have some other components of your fear of criticism and condemnation.


## How to help yourself?

Accept imperfection. The world is not ideal and neither are we. You have the right to make mistakes. Many times criticism helps to discover errors that we did not notice; This is an opportunity to do something better.

Accept that we do not have to live up to the expectations of others. If a loved one or partner truly means well, they will accept them for their mistakes and flaws.

Seek support and help from like-minded people. The world is full of people who criticize sports.

Don't be afraid to respond to criticism - this is an additional opportunity to prove your worth and professionalism. When receiving criticism ask yourself: what of this can I take away and what can I leave behind?

Choose a suitable time to read reviews when you are in a calm state. Reading critical comments in a state of excitement, for example, immediately after a speech, is more likely to make you feel "overwhelmed" by emotions.

If you receive negative reviews or comments, it's a good sign: you've been noticed!

# Chapter 6
# How to overcome
# the feeling of guilt

Therapists, when working with guilt, have to deal with each patient's traumas so that expectations (both good and bad) can be released so that forgiveness can occur. Since emotions are a form of psychic energy, they obey the laws of energy transformation and therefore cannot be destroyed. They can only be transformed, and anger and guilt must be transformed into love for complete healing to occur. The therapist's job is to help transform this energy.

## How to recognize feelings of guilt

The feeling of guilt has many faces and, in addition to the direct feeling of "your fault", it takes different forms.

### • Apologies

First, notice if you have a habit of apologizing too much. "Excuse me, can I come in?", "Please forgive me if I am taking up your time." In such situations, by using an apology, we try to soften our intervention, although this can be done with other forms of politeness.

If you are familiar with this behavior, try to think about why you are apologizing.

The mechanism of inappropriate and disproportionate apologies for the situation can also be used by people prone to blaming themselves.

**• The attitude of "I don't deserve happiness"**

A chronic feeling of your "badness", or the inconsistency of ideals (invented by yourself or instilled by other people) may indicate that you are controlled by a feeling of guilt. It makes you think that you are not worthy of praise, a happy life, or anything you want.

An example is the continuation of an unhappy relationship or marriage "for the sake of the children" ("so as not to upset the mother", "to preserve the union"), "a positive image in the eyes of others." For these people, the idea of being able to defend their interests and be happy is almost sinful, because their well-being takes last place among all other "most important" motives.

Existing next to a person not loved for some higher goal is a clear reflection of the internal attitude "I am not worthy of happiness", which is directly related to feelings of guilt.

**•     Assault**

The other pole of guilt is aggression directed both at others and at oneself.

Blame aggression is an unexpressed complaint against an aggressor who once damaged your self-esteem and positive self-perception. Here we are talking about unconscious perception, and if you certainly cannot say what the problem is, then the conflict remains in your psyche and all its participants with their roles are perpetuated on an unconscious level.

If after the conflict there was no "revenge" (for example, a constructive confrontation), it is likely that the subconscious desire to punish the enemy will follow you until you find a way out.

Clear examples of overt aggression include the habit of criticizing others and the desire to be right, to have the last word in any situation. This behavior is typical of those people who internally despise the right to make mistakes, and who consider even their most insignificant imperfection a weakness. By criticizing others, people often avoid the risk that someone, in their opinion, can see their imperfections. They seem to attack first. Or they demand too much from themselves, follow them strictly, and cannot forgive others for different behavior.

So if you make a habit of criticizing others (whether silently or out loud), remember the feeling you get when you do it. Try to understand why this feeling is useful to you, what it brings, and why you need to experience it again and again.

Very often, feelings of guilt are accompanied by unexpressed aggression. If in the case of the habit of criticizing we see its obvious manifestation, then repressed aggression is not so simple. It can take the form of mild hostility (for example, some people become angry in a stressful situation), conflict at work, aggressive driving style, that is, those manifestations of which a person is usually aware and has learned to control. But sometimes repressed emotions can manifest themselves in paradoxical ways.

For example, excessive kindness or fear of expressing dissatisfaction, fear of defending your needs, getting your way, or having a constructive discussion. The fear of expressing aggression (and, possibly, receiving it directed at you) and the inability to express it lead a person to look for ways to merge with others, to feel comfortable for others. The fear of being rejected leads to the fear of defending one's interests.

**Real and imaginary guilt**

Real guilt is a feeling of remorse that is the psychological consequence of an action or inaction that has negative consequences for other people, or oneself.

Real guilt can be deontological (referring to the duty to do), resulting from a violation of one's values or morals. Another type of guilt is altruistic, which arises from causing harm to other people.

If the guilt is really real, to alleviate the condition and atone for the guilt, the following measures should be taken, with the help of a psychologist, a spiritual advisor, or on your own:

• Recognize the fact of causing harm to other people, animals, society, etc.
• Find and recognize the reasons for actions or inactions.

• Come to sincere repentance (usually with the help of a counselor),
• Express the intention to cancel or compensate for the damage caused,
• Atone for harm caused by actual actions or compensate for it indirectly.
• Refuse to self-punish for "sins" and not allow anyone to punish you (except by judicial decision). To stop self-punishment, you may need the help of a psychologist.
• Regain self-respect, lost as a result of all of the above.

## Real guilt denied or repressed

In this case, as a result of the action of primitive psychological defense mechanisms, the real guilt is not recognized and therefore is repressed. In this case, responsibility for one's actions is not accepted and many times one's guilt is projected onto others. This mechanism is implemented due to the traumatized and surviving part of the personality of self-sabotage. The main task of the sabotage part is to protect the injured part of the personality – the victim – from repeated contact with the trauma. Therefore, the Saboteur does everything possible to prevent the injured party from coming into contact with the blame. It is typical of those people:

• Rejection and denial of the existence of guilt
• Lack of conscience as a moral regulator of behavior.
• Denial of existing moral, ethical and legal norms ("my life is my rules")
• Manifestations of aggression towards any obstacle on the way to the goal.

• Does not consider it necessary to take into account the interests of other people.
• Creates his philosophy of life ("sovereign") that justifies his actions.

Therapy in these cases is extremely difficult. However, in some cases it is possible to help the patient express repressed feelings of guilt and, through sincere repentance, regain a sense of self-esteem.

Imaginary guilt is almost more common than real guilt. Furthermore, if real guilt can be atoned for, then it will only be possible to get rid of imaginary guilt during psychotherapy.


## Psychological help with imaginary guilt

If you cannot get rid of the real guilt yourself or with professional help; It will be very difficult to do so with imaginary guilt, since, without knowing the true causes of imaginary guilt, you will not be able to get rid of it.

A therapist can help you find and understand the true causes of guilt and show you the futility of investing in this feeling and the strategy of self-punishment. With an imaginary fault of birth, the patient is exempt from responsibility for her birth. At the same time, the person is helped to accept themselves as born worthy of living without conditions, as if they had an unconditional right to life and to be themselves.

In case of guilt caused by parental instructions, the patient is released from parental drivers and prohibitions and is given constructive counter-instructions. If necessary, work is done to repair and create a loving parent within oneself for one's inner child.


## What is forgiveness?

Forgiveness is a universal way to release resentment, guilt, and anger. Forgiveness does not mean releasing another or oneself from responsibility. Accountability and reparation for actual harm must be separated from forgiveness. "Forgiving" means releasing the demands and expectations one places on others or oneself and releasing anger repressed or held in resentment. This fixation of resentment and anger consumes a person's resources and hinders his or her personal growth and development. In addition, unexpressed anger and the expectation of punishment for the offender lead to the formation of psychological dependence of the accuser on the accused.

Forgiveness does not mean forgetting the past and does not mean justifying actions. Forgiveness comes from finding and dealing with hidden expectations in oneself or others. At the same time, some of these expectations that a person has may be completely reasonable and normal. However, they did not come true and probably never will come true. Eliminating expectations frees up mental energy consumed by repressed anger and other negative emotions associated with guilt. Forgiveness results in the willingness to take responsibility for oneself and allow others to take responsibility for themselves.

## Consequences of not forgiving

• Refusing to forgive someone will allow you to justify her inaction and reject responsibility.
• The refusal to forgive excuses the lack of self-development and work on oneself.
• Refusing to forgive allows you to receive sympathy as a victim and manipulate others.
• Holding on to anger creates a false sense of power when it takes more courage and strength to let it go and transform it into love.

## Forgiveness of others and self-forgiveness scenario

Think about painful events or situations that make you angry at yourself or others.

Dig deeper into your memories and uncover the hidden expectations associated with these situations. Notice how parts of your personality (who is inside you) may be the sources or carriers of these expectations.

Imagine the object of your resentment and anger in front of you (yourself or someone else).

Address him with the following words, preferably out loud:
• "I choose not to punish myself or feel hurt or upset about what you did (or didn't do)."

• I would prefer that you say (or not say), do (or not do) the following ________________________________.

• But you didn't (couldn't) do it and I can't influence it. Therefore, I choose the following: I cancel all demands, expectations, and conditions that I proposed to you for ________________________________, then and now. I remove the requirement that you behave, think, and feel a certain way. (You are fully responsible for your actions and actions).

• I accept you as you are. (In the case of working with ourselves, we add - I love you and I accept you as you are without conditions).

Then become aware of your body, feel how you feel, and whether you are holding on to some expectations or demanding that someone be different. If the body does not feel liberated and bodily symptoms appear, repeat the process, advancing the process for each sensation detected in the body. Each expectation and each complaint must be considered separately.

Sometimes you have to work with a subpersonality that has confused the expectation of retribution and anger in its life script. This scenario can be identified by asking part of the personality what would happen if they let go of their expectations. The answer could be: "I would become nobody", "I would become vulnerable", or "It would be ridiculous".

## How to get out of the vicious circle and stop pleasing people?

First of all, you must learn to accept yourself as you are and accept and appreciate your interests and needs. And, secondly, it is enough to stop pleasing others, surpassing their interests. Through a series of simple steps, self-confidence and self-esteem will progressively increase:

Even if you feel like you should always say "yes," remember that you also have the right to say "no" or not respond at all. Always remember to say "no" to anything undesirable - it's about setting personal boundaries that protect your autonomy and self-identity. By refusing to spend your precious time on undesirable things, you will soon discover that it is much easier than suffering over something you don't like. You will be surprised, but over time, those around you will begin to value you more: people who value themselves and their time command more respect than always agreeing with everything.

Saying no is the hardest thing the first time. Justify your refusal with a good reason, but never go into details so as not to make excuses: You are not to blame for anything! Therefore, he refuses quickly and unequivocally, without verbosity, without attempting to defend his decision.

Be confident in what you say: make a decision and don't change it. This gives the impression that you have preferences, even if you don't yet.
The next time you are asked to help with someone else's work or project, think about your work and your

concerns. You don't have to agree just to get approval. Remember what is important to you.

At first, all these steps can generate remorse and feelings of guilt. You may feel selfish and that you are focusing only on yourself and your needs. There is no need to break. Calm down and if you want to help others, set a strict deadline for doing so. For example, let's say you'll only have two hours from 6:00 p.m. to 8:00 p.m. or so. This will allow you to manage your time and not refuse help if someone needs it.

Instead of doing what others want, you should focus on who you are and what you want to achieve in your life. When meeting the needs of others becomes your only goal in life, you will simply lose yourself. So, try to figure out what you like to do.

Whenever someone asks you for a favor, it's okay to say that they should think before making a promise. This extra time will give you a chance to think so you can decide without compromising your interests.

Always think about whether you want to do what you are asked to do. Think about how difficult it will be to do something against your own will and how relieved you will feel when you refuse to do something against your will. Try to make a list of actions you need to take, those you are normally asked to do, and those you can refuse.

Don't overdo it, be smart, because if you reject all kinds of help or meetings with others due to your laziness or for the pure pleasure of being alone, then when you need others or want company and others reject you, it will be too late. Live in a society with norms of empathy, cooperation, and reciprocity, not as a castaway on an island.

Always check the offers that other people make you. See if they can do it all on their own, but still ask you for help. If you are being manipulated, you have every right to refuse to help.

Sometimes it is not necessary to answer anything. Silence, an eloquent smile, or a look may be enough to refuse. In this case, the manipulator will perfectly understand that you have decided not to give in to him.

Remember, people always need to feel heard and understood. So even if you are going to say no, be respectful and do it politely. In the past, in this case, there was a delicious formulation for the negative: "Positively, no!"

When your boss makes a request, you don't have to refuse. But if the request comes from a colleague, don't back down if he can say no. This way, it will be easy for you to stop being a people-pleaser.

If he feels guilty about the rejection, remember that he cannot be responsible for everything that happens. He never promised that he would take care of everything in life, everyone around him to the detriment of himself.
Take care of yourself, reward yourself, and support yourself for every achievement. Become his best friend who treats him the way he deserves.

Listen to what his inner self says and always talk to yourself about your own needs. Practice spending some quiet time with yourself during the day.

If you still find it difficult to change your attitude towards a problem, if your uncertainty prevents you from being alone and making your own decisions, it is always advisable to seek psychological help.

In emotional-imaginative therapy, the desire to please is seen as a sign of an experienced, but not lived, psychological trauma that led to the division of the traumatized Inner Child into separate structures, some of which adopted a survival strategy through rescue and pleasure. To understand the reasons for such behavior, which takes away a person's resources, does not allow him to live his own life fully, develop and grow as an individual, and build harmonious relationships with other people, it is necessary to find primary and repeated injuries. Its nature must be understood and treated. As we free ourselves from coping mechanisms in trauma, which include agreeable behavior, as the integrity of a person's original true nature is restored, their self-awareness and behavior will change, and their own previously lost strengths and resources. They will return, the ability to feel will return, and the need for behavior that attempts to keep the person from turning inward will recede.

## Why you should get rid of guilt

The feeling of guilt devours a person's resources because he has to dedicate his vital energy to "attend" to this problem.

Living with a feeling of guilt is extremely costly and at some point can lead to collapse, so it is very important to deal with the disturbing symptoms and resolve them on your own or in psychotherapy. These symptoms include nervous breakdowns, alcohol and drug abuse, chronic illnesses, and many other manifestations that make life difficult, poor, and unhappy.

Since we are talking about unconscious processes, changes must occur there. The most effective way is, of course, psychotherapy: short or long-term, individual or group; Your wishes can be discussed with a psychologist or therapist who, after understanding your request and compiling an anamnesis (information provided by the patient and other testimonies to compile your medical history), will propose a treatment regimen.

To understand the problem yourself, you can use various approaches from cognitive psychology.

• Write down under what circumstances and with what people you feel guilty most often.

• Write and analyze: are there similarities in these situations and people? And then remember if a similar situation happened to you before. Perhaps in your childhood or adolescence.

• When you are trapped in this experience, try to control what happens to you physically and psychologically. Notice the reactions of your body and mind. Developing this sensitivity helps learn to separate yourself from your reactions and, ultimately, manage them.

• Do self-training with yourself. Remember that the situation occurred in the past and, although it extends to the present, you do not need to follow this scenario.

• Tell yourself more often that there is no ideal world, no ideal situations, and certainly no ideal people. The desire to be perfect leads to neurosis. The optimal thing is to strive to be good enough and give yourself room for error.

• Remember that you are in control and that you can overcome suffering in many ways.

It is important to carry out these practices carefully and constantly to notice positive changes over time.

Finally, I would like to talk about a very common mechanism that almost all people use when trying to understand what is happening inside them. This is an intellectualization and rationalization of one's condition, an attempt to live, not with feelings and emotions, but with the "head."

Of course, reflection is good. The ability to be aware and reflect on internal processes is an excellent skill that helps in many life situations. But it is important to note the moment when the thought process has become routine and does not provide real relief.

Thinking a lot and for a long time about a problem does not mean solving it, and often means the opposite ("I prefer to think about it than act").

Our thinking apparatus has nothing to do with the sensory sphere, and its "pump" is good for understanding the problem and developing a strategy for solving it. But the decision itself always falls into the realm of feelings and emotions. This is what a psychologist or psychotherapist focuses on: he invites you to explore together another side of your personality: unconscious feeling processes that were once damaged by trauma and have not yet received the attention they deserve.


**Operating procedure in therapy**

The goal of psychological work with the experience of guilt is to experience it emotionally as fully as possible, complete the experience, determine which norms were violated, and realize the discrepancy between one's ideas about norms and the real norms operating in society. Identify the actual victim, determine the actual degree of his or her guilt, decide if it is possible to atone or correct the harm caused, discover how it can be done, and implement the plan. The result of the work must be repentance, apology, and atonement as a way of returning to "real people." Thus, guilt becomes the experience of experiencing oneself as a person, part of society, bearer of norms and rules.

## Stages of working with guilt in psychological counseling

### 1. Definition of the client's current state as an experience of guilt.

Most of the time this is obvious, but sometimes the experience of guilt is identified by the following signs:

• Persistent self-accusation,
• Unreasonable and obsessive insults against oneself,
• An inexplicable decrease in self-esteem and a feeling of lack of freedom, deprivation of one's own will.

One of the most striking signs of a pathological and painful experience of guilt is the inability to apologize. The person feels so overwhelmed by guilt that they are unable to consciously accept the blame and say "I'm sorry" or "It's my fault." Growing and painful resentment can also be a sign of chronic guilt since resentment is an obligatory part of guilt.

Another undoubted sign (and source) of guilt is pronounced perfectionism, that is, the desire to do everything perfectly. Such a person does not forgive himself for his mistakes, inaccuracies, and ignorance. That's why he always has reasons to accuse himself.

A simplified and unrealistic image of the Self cannot, in general, be considered a sign of guilt. But, without a doubt, it is accompanied by a feeling of guilt. This self-image is especially typical of adolescents. A simplified image of the Self is usually schematic, monochromatic, and has great elasticity, that is, immutability. Interestingly, a constant feeling of guilt accompanies both schematically positive and schematically negative self-images.

A schematically positive image of "I" can be roughly characterized by the following phrases: "I am a good person, I am decent and honest, intelligent, I know everything, I cannot make mistakes, I have no bad thoughts." With this image of the Self, any mistake or even situational anger becomes the basis for a painful experience of guilt. The most unpleasant thing is that these experiences do not find a way out and accumulate because to repent and forgive oneself it is necessary to change the image of the Self and include in it the concept of one's imperfection.

Schematically, the negative image of the "I" can be characterized by the following phrases: "I am a loser, I never succeed in anything, I will ruin everything." With this image of the Self, a person will feel guilty, even if he did nothing or did something good. In the first case, due to inaction, and in the second, due to not taking something into account or not being able to reproduce a positive result in the future. These people experience their victories as undeserved luck or as a victory taken from another.

Another situation in which it is necessary to suspect a deep and constant feeling of guilt is the case in which a person considers himself "different", "not human" and perhaps even a monster. These people often feel deeper guilt, mixed with shame, when faced with any type of openness or close contact with others. Interestingly, even those who consider themselves better than others can feel guilty. Monstrosity is not necessary here either, it is enough to feel like the "ugly duckling" of the family.

There are also external signs that a person is experiencing guilt: facial: frozen expression of pain, pronounced vegetative-vascular changes (redness and pallor), clenched hands, compressed posture, facial expressions, and pantomime of tension and fear. It is worth mentioning that psychosomatic manifestations such as migraines, back pain, abdominal pain, and gastrointestinal problems can be manifestations of habitual or unexperienced feelings of guilt. In addition, external signs of a feeling of guilt can be impulsive or even compulsive actions of a person: obsessive apologies, constant self-justifications, readiness to accept blame without reasoning, restlessness, and servility.

Of course, any difficult experience is framed individually for each person. Some experience it vividly, others erase it; Our goal in this case is to point out possible signs. Modern trends in the development of society suggest a change in attitude towards the experience of feelings of guilt; Generally speaking, it is not fashionable to experience feelings of guilt and does not correspond to the trends of globalization and liberalization. It is curious, but this is true: when the social context expands and the category "we" is excluded from it, the feeling of guilt is inappropriate and must be erased. If the trends continue, this will certainly lead to a change in facial and pantomime signs of guilt, and suppression of expression, but will not (we hope) affect the experience itself.

## 2. Rehabilitation of the experience of guilt.

The patient (and the psychologist) needs to change her attitude toward the experience of guilt. The easiest way to do this is to convince the person that the painful experience of guilt has a very specific positive function (connection with the deceased, maintenance of self-esteem, ability to legally experience negative feelings, etc.). The function must be determined for a given situation and a specific person.

For example, the memory of a cruel act against a weak person makes the person especially sensitive to such situations. The heavy experience of guilt for his cruelty, for the pleasure received during the harassment, for his sense of power, becomes a constant reminder of the inadmissibility of such behavior, of his rejection, and a powerful means of regulating subsequent behavior. It does not allow one to adopt a position of sinlessness and holiness. Such a person can become a defender of the weak. It also happens that the feeling of guilt reminds us of a past act, which for some reason cannot be completely forgotten. Guilt plays the role of a buoy on an important event that has sunk into the abyss of the unconscious. Simply dismissing this feeling without analyzing it is missing an important opportunity.

It's quite difficult to accept this: the guilt feels too painful. Additionally, the client (and the psychologist) must believe that feelings of guilt can lead to resolution and relief.

Almost everyone over the age of 10 has the experience of positive resolution of guilt, the soul-cleansing experience of repentance, apology, and forgiveness, but sometimes these experiences are difficult to remember. If you can explain to the client the important positive function of guilt and the possibility of getting rid of it "for good", it will be much easier to convince him to analyze the guilt and deal with it. Practice shows that any experience that has become chronic, any mental stereotype recorded in experiences or behaviors, even pathological ones, plays an important role.

Trying to get rid of something without understanding why we have it can have very dire consequences.


## 3. Resources
If the client is willing to explore his guilt, before doing anything else, he should make sure that he is capable of doing so. That is, we must take care of resources. The analysis of feelings of guilt should be carried out if you have time, health, and strength. If there is neither one nor the other, nor the third, and it is necessary to analyze the feeling of guilt, then it is necessary to at least train the client to resort to his resources. There are many techniques for this: breathing techniques, visualizations, the ability to ask for help and support, use of psychological assistance resources (services, literature, etc.). Starting this process, it is necessary to remember that the consciousness of guilt often comes suddenly, falls on a person, permeates his entire being, and is not always in the therapist's office, so a person must be ready to help himself. herself through this. crisis. Or at least know its possibility.

## 4. Work with feelings of guilt

1) **Reconstruction of a situation in which a person did wrong**. Sometimes there are several, in which case you have to move on from the most recent or the brightest. Very often it makes sense to practice the technology of analyzing guilt in a situation that is not the most significant. Here it is necessary to remember that a complete reconstruction of the situation is needed with all the motives and experiences at the time of the action. Often, the basis for feeling guilt is not the act itself, but a feeling that does not correspond to our ideas about ourselves. For example, a mother may feel wracked with guilt because she did not feel sorry for her child's crying. Although her behavior was impeccable, she reproaches herself for feelings of irritation, hostility, and indifference.

2) **Determination of the true victim.** It happens that with chronic or inveterate guilt, not only the violated norm is "replaced" in conscience, but also the person against whom the wrong action was committed. For analysis, it is necessary to reconstruct the real victim and the real actions so that an apology or atonement brings true relief. An apology for a minor offense and compensation directed to the uninjured bring no relief.

3) **It is necessary to find and formulate exactly what social norm was violated and determine how it differs from the person's internal norms.** For example, a mother who is irritated or even very angry with her child believes that she is violating the norm "A good mother should always love her child" or "normal mothers should always be happy only with her child.""".

This norm is unrealistic and for a living person, it will always be a basis for self-accusation. But in this case, it is useless to appeal to external norms ("everyone does it", "it is impossible", etc.). An unrealistic standard is still a standard; It cannot be changed so easily and we must work with it. It may weaken if a woman is convinced by her own experience that others do not follow her. Then she can change it, for example, to this: "Love allows for different feelings." Or it may happen that the victim is not this mother's real child, but her inner child, whom she once promised not to yell at her future children. From this point of view, the rule is quite realistic (and we wanted to discuss it and change it immediately!). Awareness of this norm makes the feeling of guilt normal, and logical, and the process of forming internal norms understandable and partially manageable.

4) **It is necessary to relive and experience the entire complex of emotional experiences that arose after the commission of the act.** This means that you should name all the feelings experienced at that moment (anger, shame, anger, shock, fear, resentment, etc.), and try to talk about each of them. If talking and naming do not bring relief, then it is necessary to find the cause and time of appearance of each of these feelings. This seems very difficult, but it comes naturally with a fairly good reconstruction of the situation. It must be remembered that almost all of these feelings need legalization. As a result of this process, the patient may realize that he had a reason to experience these feelings and that they were necessary for him.

Of particular importance at this stage is working with resentment, which is an integral part of the experience of guilt. As a rule, resentment arises when you feel guilty: against yourself - "for such a stupid setup"; about the partner - for putting him in such a situation; about the group, society, or destiny, for the possibility of creating such a situation, such difficult experiences. If he does not address the offense and move past it, he will not be able to fully overcome the guilt.

If the process progresses successfully, most of the experiences already in this stage fade away and are no longer painful. Minor faults and harmless offenses do not require any additional action, because the person repents of them automatically and unconsciously. Later stages are necessary for those who cannot do this.


## 5. Repentance.
This is internal work, working with feelings. Questions of actions and behavior arise only after repentance.

**The first stage** is a complete description of what the client did to the other person. For example: "When the older kids bullied the little boy, I stood next to him and did nothing to protect him." It is very important to formulate this description precisely in terms of action. It will not be possible to repent of an offense expressed in a global value judgment, such as "I ruined your life," or "I betrayed your trust."

**The second stage** is the recognition and description of the feelings and reasons that caused the patient to act in this way. For example: "I was very afraid, I was glad that it was him, and not me, who was in his place, I felt sorry for the boy, but I was afraid that if he intervened, they would change me." The important thing to remember here is that everything must be formulated in the form of statements. Otherwise, everything will simply become a torrent of accusations, self-justifications, or self-recriminations.

**The third stage** is the formulated norm that was violated. For example: "We must protect the weak", "we must overcome our fear", and "You cannot rejoice in the pain of others." Sometimes this rule may seem quite strange, for example: "You can't talk back to adults", "You can't shout", or "You can't walk barefoot". An internal standard can be any statement. You can't argue with him.

**The fourth stage** is taking responsibility for your actions. For example: "It is my fault for not helping this child and giving in to my fear." Phrases formulated at this stage may also seem quite strange, for example: "I couldn't defend myself against an adult aggressor." Even if the statement sounds crazy, you shouldn't try to rephrase it on your own. There is always logic inside, but often it is not visible from the outside. An indicator of the correctness of the formulation is the relief immediately after saying it out loud.

**The fifth stage** is the search and clarification of other behavioral options that the client would consider acceptable for himself at that moment with the reconstruction of the possible consequences of this type of action, for example: "I could throw something heavy at them and run away. As they walked away, they ran after me and left the child alone. It would be the right thing to do, but it would be very dangerous", "I could run to find one of the adults and bring him to help him", "I could approach this child later when everything is over." "Come and try to comfort him." These actions may seem strange and meaningless, but finding different ways to resolve a hopeless situation in the past gives a surprisingly positive effect (this is how they often work in case of trauma): it expands a person's capabilities, and relieves feelings of hopelessness and helplessness. and changes a person's thinking and behavior in similar situations. This procedure leaves the person with a positive experience of overcoming a negative situation, which in reality they did not have, and exempts them from responsibility for impossible actions.


**6. Apologies or atonement.**
After a person has repented, the question arises of what he should do now with his repentance.

1) If it is possible to apologize to the person the client is guilty of, then it is better to do so. In this case, the apology must be rehearsed. Ideally, the apology formula should contain in one form or another the following formulas (simultaneously or sequentially):

• "I am guilty before you because I did..."
• "I did this because I... (I was afraid, I didn't understand, I was angry, etc.)"
• "It is very unpleasant for me, I am very sorry, I regret it..."
• "What can I do for you to make up for my guilt?"

We must remember that an apology is always the beginning of a dialogue, not its end. The person to whom we apologize may accept the apology, may not accept it immediately, or may not accept it at all. Apologizing does not guarantee our forgiveness, but it certainly alleviates the feeling of guilt, transferring it from a purely internal experience to a process of communication.

2) If the client does not have a real opportunity to apologize, you must find atonement for his guilt, for example, helping someone in a similar situation. This is not always easy to do, but if desired, it is very possible. These actions bring unconditional relief and benefit.

3) The purpose of atonement is to correct the harm caused or make the situation impossible in the future. It is easy to atone for material guilt; This usually means replacing the damaged item or compensating the damage with money. Atoning for psychological damage is much more difficult and increasingly involves dialogue with the victim. Atonement for psychological harm is healing trauma through empathy and compassion.

4) Sometimes the question of punishment arises. If punishment is imposed by society, then the psychological task is to correlate it with a feeling of guilt and internally convert it into atonement. If society is not directly involved in the process and the punishment exists in the form of self-punishment, then the psychological task is to make the process logical, associated with guilt and the corresponding rules. If a person beats himself to bruises after yelling

at a child, then it is worth giving him at least safer ways (doing push-ups, for example), and then legalizing all the accompanying feelings and seeking atonement for the damage caused. the child and himself.


#######